Release It!
Workbook

Release It! - Workbook

The Key to True Freedom

Cover design & Layout by: C. D. Johnson
www.diverseskillcenter.com

Printed in the United States of America

ISBN-13: 978-1530886944 ISBN-10: 1530886945

Table of Contents

LESSON TOPIC 1.1
Introduction of Moral/Spiritual Injury

Objective: Individuals will have a better understanding of the two injuries and how they can and will have an effect in their daily living.

Defining Moral and Spiritual.
Injury are they the same?

In the context of war, moral injuries may stem from direct participation in acts of combat, such as killing or harming others, or indirect acts, such as witnessing death or dying, failing to prevent immoral acts of others, or giving or receiving orders that are perceived as gross moral violations. The act may have been carried out by an individual or a group through a decision made individually or as a response to orders given by leaders.

Like psychological trauma, moral injury is a construct that describes extreme and unprecedented life experiences including the harmful aftermath of exposure to such events. Events are considered morally injurious if they "transgress deeply held moral beliefs and expectations". Thus, the key precondition for moral injury is an act of transgression, which shatters moral and ethical expectations that are rooted in religious or spiritual beliefs, or culture-based, organizational, and group-based rules about fairness, the value of life, and so forth (www.ptsd.va.gov).

Spirituality is a personal experience with many definitions. Spirituality might be defined as "an inner belief system providing an individual with meaning and purpose in life, a sense of the sacredness of life, and a vision for the betterment of the world". Other definitions emphasize "a connection to that which transcends the self". The connection might be to God, a higher power, a universal energy, the sacred, or to nature. Researchers in the field of spirituality have suggested three useful dimensions for thinking about one's spirituality:
- Beliefs
- Spiritual Practices
- Spiritual Experiences

5

LESSON TOPIC 2.1
The Connections of the Symptom to the Moral/Spiritual Injury

OBJECTIVE
Learn how to recognize and trace from fruit (symptoms) to root injuries by.

Listening with the mind

Discerning cause and effect

Listening with the Heart

Listening to Higher Power

The most common spiritual roots, by far, are unforgiveness and bitterness strongholds, lodged in the heart, as a result of judging with condemnation, resentment or dishonor. Studies show most people who quit their jobs leave because they cannot get along with others.

DISCERNING (Exercise)

Transgressed acts may result in highly aversive and haunting states of inner conflict and turmoil

Listening with our minds for surface patterns = Surface symptoms
(Example: biting of nails, appearance)

_____

_____

_____

_____

_____

_____

_____

_____

_____

_____

_____

_____

_____

_____

_____

_____

_____

_____

Discerning causes/effect in surface situations = Surface
Situations (Example: combat/loss of self = feelings of not belonging)

Listening with our hearts for the root wounds = Root symptoms
(Example: regret, guilt, shame)

_____

_____

_____

_____

_____

_____

_____

_____

_____

_____

_____

_____

_____

_____

_____

_____

_____

_____

_____

_____

Listening to the Higher power for root causes = Root causes
(Example: meditate, find quiet place)

Recognition of Fruit (Symptoms) To Root Patterns
A Prayer for Discernment

Lord, I thank You for Your word that gives me direction and understanding to discern and face the truth about myself. I ask for Your anointing to be able to recognize self-destructive habits or life patterns that produce bad fruit because of a harmful or sinful root. Bring healing and comfort for present hurts and wounds; then look with me, through the clear eyes of Your love, into my past. Show me how, where, and when this hurt began and give me the courage to confront whatever You reveal. Together, in Your power, we can overcome anything.

Help me see my sinful reactions with clarity so that the power of forgiveness can bring down the walls of resentment, anger and pain I have built. Forgive me for judging those I held responsible for aiding me in planting my sinful roots. I freely forgive anyone who nurtured or encouraged the growth of fruit that was detrimental. I forgive myself for allowing my mind and body to be led into destructive habits and life patterns.

Father, You alone can guide me through the tangled forest of my past. You have seen my life form its very beginning. Nothing surprises or shocks You, for You already know all about me and still You continue to amaze me with Your constant love.

Open my mind and my memories to discern the harmful roots in my past that have developed destructive habits or life patterns over the years, resulting in damaging or worthless fruit. Hew Your axe of grace into my harmful or sinful roots and free me to produce good fruit worthy of a child of God.

Lord, as I partner with You to minister to others, I lay everything I think I know on the altar; all my training, all my experience and every method that has worked in the past.

Open my spiritual ears to hear on 3 levels; mind, heart and spirit. Open my eyes to see past their sin to their painful wounded roots and how You want to heal them. Give me keen discernment to know how to bring them to repentance for their sinful reactions. Be that skillful detective in me that would notice what is conspicuously absent in their story.
Most of all, may I be a demonstration of Your gentleness, only offering ministry where I am clearly invited. May I be in perfect concert with Your will, Your way and Your timing. May I have the true heart of a minister who comes only to restore in humility, know except for Your grace, there go I. Amen

LESSON TOPIC 3.1

Is Meditation the Answer to Changing your Brain?

Objective: Individuals will have a better understanding of why meditation is important for better health Physically and Mentally

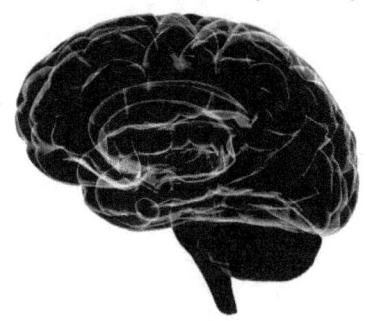

The Benefits of Meditation

Meditation has been the central practice in almost every spiritual and religious tradition for thousands of years. Regular meditation will enrich your life, develop your consciousness and cultivate abilities that will benefit you now and in the future. Some of the direct and indirect benefits of mediation are listed below:

Direct Benefits (spiritual development)
- Develops "mind" qualities such as creativity, intuition and wisdom
- Develops "heart" qualities such as compassion, courage, peace and joy
- Develops "body" qualities such as will, resilience and presence
- Systematically activates higher levels of consciousness
- Purifies awareness

Indirect Benefits (personal development)
- Psychological healing & reintegration

- Calms the body and mind, and improves the clarity of thought
- Increases feelings of peace, happiness and contentment
- Reduces stress, anxiety, depression & anger
- Subdues automatic ego reactions and conditional behaviors
- Can reduce our biological age by 5 to 10 years

LESSON TOPIC 3.1 (Exercise)
The Power of Mediation

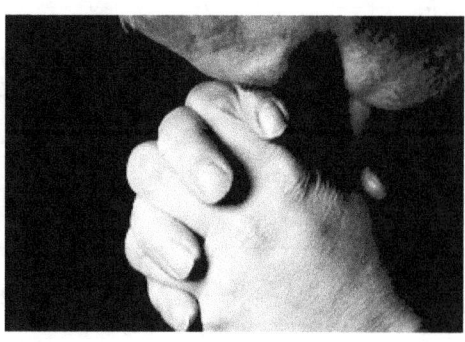

Improved
Health among
the workforce

Physical
complaints

Impulsiveness

Emotional
Instability

Tendency
Towards
Neurosis

Anxiety

Name a few ways that you have or can meditate
And give the results

_____

_____

_____

_____

_____

_____

_____

_____

_____

LESSON TOPIC 4.1
What is Truth (Real)? & What is not (Lies)?

OBJECTIVE: To learn what was the belief
That occurred during the traumatic
Experience and measure its validly to
What really happen.

"And you shall know the truth, and the truth
shall make you free. John 8:32

MAGICAL THINKING
ABOUT HOW TO MOVE

COMMON MYTHS

Magical Thinking

- Just forget about it
- Stuff it and put on happy face
- Confess that I am fine or ok until my confession feels like it is actually the truth
- Act out violent actions of words against inanimate objects, in order to weaken negative emotions
- Say what others want to hear or do what others want me to do, protecting their emotions first.
- Give others a piece of my mind judge, accuse or blame while my negative feelings are still intense enough

_____

_____

_____

_____

_____

_____

LESSON TOPIC 4.1 Exercise
What is The Injury Behind the Reaction?

If someone said or did a certain thing that ticked me off, a trigger mechanism would go off and unhealed traumatic memories would flood my mind (and I would experience the emotions related to the event of a particular memory).

The Deadly Two Forces that Work Together
It has been discovered through research and actual case studies that thoughts carry more power activity than sound waves emitted form a local radio or television station. Thoughts are very powerful, but words are even MORE powerful.

Exercise: Do you know what was the Lie and what was the Truth?

Truth

_____

_____

_____

_____

_____

_____

_____

Continuation of Exercise

Lies

LESSON TOPIC 4.2

Who do you see when you look in the mirror?

Perception plays a big role in what we believe

Example: A lady, a high school teacher, had a regular practice of walking into her classroom and putting her books down, open the desk drawer for pencils and other things, and then begin the class. The students decided to have some fun and play a trick on her. So they put a rubber snake inside the drawer. When she did her usual thing and because of the movement of the drawer, the rubber snake wiggled. She thought it was a real snake and she screamed, she fainted and had a critical heart attack. This is to show that the rubber snake, even though it was fake, as long as she thought it was a real snake, was real to her. And so her perception was reality.

What we see and hear can mislead us

Example: A survivor of childhood abuse may act as if she believes no matter what she does she is not safe because when she was a child that was true. However, while she can speak words saying she will not let anyone hurt her the fruit of her life tells a different story, as she gets involved in one abusive relationship after another.

_____

_____

_____

_____

_____

_____

_____

_____

SPIRITUAL BLOCKS:

Bitterroot Expectations and Judgement, Unforgiveness

If you are not careful this could be you.

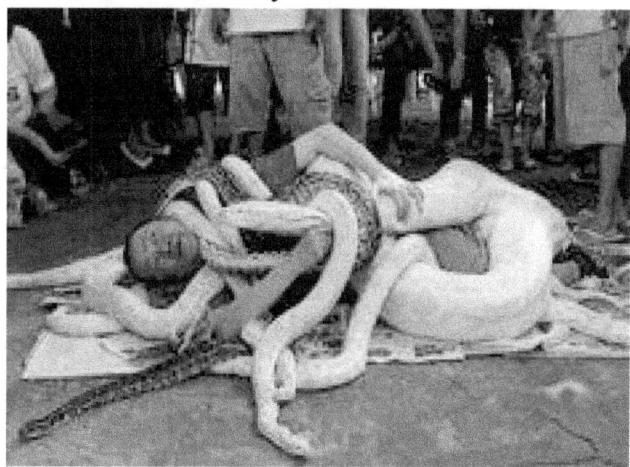

OBJECTIVE: To learn discomfort of discontent, longing envy, jealousy, anger, compulsion, and anxiety can contaminate your life, tighten your body and constrict your heart.

As you can see roots tend to get tangled when not paid attention to.

Man's Soul Has Three Parts

What lies in the soul of a man? Love, Laughter, Heartache, Sorrow? Pride, Fear, Rage and Contentment? The true measure of a man lies in his heart and in his soul. The soul, the person of man, is likewise composed of three parts: the mind, the will and the emotion.

When we look at Scriptures it identifies the mind as a part of the soul. A good example of this is in the Psalms, I will praise You, for I am awesomely and wonderfully made: Your works are wonderful, and my soul knows it well. Psalms 139:14

To know knowledge, it has to pertain to the **mind**. Lamentations 3:20 says, My **soul** remembers them well and is bowed down within me. To remember is another function of the **mind**. These verses clearly indicate that there is a part of the **soul** that knows and remembers: this part is the **mind**.

This will is also a part of the soul. Job had much to say about the will. For example, so that my soul would choose strangulation and death rather than my bones (Job 7:15). He also said, my soul refuses to touch them (6:7). Both choosing and refusing are functions of the will, a part of the soul.

Finally, we can see from the word that the emotion is part of the **soul**. In Songs of Solomon 1:17, the Shulamite speaks to her beloved. Tell me, you whom my soul loves. Second Samuel 5:8 records the opposite feeling: and David said on that day, whoever would strike the Jebrusites, let him go up to the water course and strike the lame and the blind, who are hated by David's **soul**. Later David experienced a change in feelings: because the soul of our

servant to rejoice since love, hate and rejoicing are clearly expressions of the emotions, it is obvious that the third emotions is the third faculty of the **soul**.

IT IS TIME TO LAY SOME THINGS TO REST

_____

_____

_____

_____

_____

_____

LESSON TOPIC 6.0
Shattering Your Strongholds

Prayer to Forgive Others and Asking Forgiveness 5 Ways
Today, right now, I am choosing to forgive, to reach ahead toward healing but Father, I do not know how to make forgiveness happen. My emotions are raw and bleeding right now. I am afraid to trust and leave my heart open to be hurt again. But I know true forgiveness is a conscious choice, not an emotion. I can choose to forgive, even if my feelings tells me I do not want to or cannot. Please give me the willingness and the inner resolve to keep on choosing to forgive until it becomes real to me and is accomplished in me by your power.

Like a wounded child, let me nestle into Your lap for comfort. Salve my bruised emotions and my aching heart. Pour in Your love until there is no room for my own self-pity. Father I choose to release all the bitterness stored in my heart against those who have hurt me, whether intentionally or not.

Show me where I need to seek forgiveness. Show me if even 10% of this conflict is my fault and what needs to be dealt with in my heart. Protect me form any sense of false guilt, if reconciliation is not possible.

Forgive me for all my sinful responses and actions against those who hurt me. Your word teaches that You can forgive me because the price for my forgiveness has already been paid by the death of Your son. This holds true as I choose to forgive others as well. The price has been paid in full by the blood of Jesus Christ.

Lord, please forgive me for projecting onto You my childish pictures of what a father is or should be. Enlighten the eyes of my heart to see You and love You as You really are, and to follow You with child-like trust, resting in Your protection.

I also forgive myself for clutching resentment, wearing my victim hood like a medal. I forgive myself for believing Satan's deception. By Your resurrection power within me, I break off the chains of resentment or bitterness that bind my heart and mind. I choose to be free. In Jesus mighty name.

LESSON TOPIC 6.1
Hearts of Stone, Walls and Inner Vows

Objective: To learn the power of words that we speak over ourselves and how they can make you a prisoner.

LESSON TOPIC 6.1 Prayer

Prayer to Break Vows, Walls, and Heart of Stones

All knowing

Show me how I have walled out meaningful relationships and help me to receive the ministry healing I need. I forgive myself for blocking satisfying relationships and apply the blood of Jesus to my sinful reactions. I forgive those who have hurt and wronged me. Lord, I ask you to forgive me for judging others with condemnation. Please forgive me for blaming You, Lord, when my relationships don't work.

I bring my fleshly protective structures to the foot of the cross and ask You to bring the whole structures to death. Remove the walls I have built and give me a heart of flesh. Lord, connect me with a spiritual authority who will pray with me to break the power of the fleshly inner vows I have made. Release me to be led of the Holy Spirit in all relationships and to rest in Your discernment and Your choices for me.

I repent and ask your forgiveness for blocking Your work in my life and for blocking others. Please restore the blessings and rewards that I have caused myself and others to miss. I choose to give you access to all my relationships and pray for healing for our bodies, minds and emotions. In Jesus' name, Amen!

_____

_____

_____

_____

_____

_____

_____

_____

_____

_____

_____

_____

_____

LESSON TOPIC 6.1
Exercise

Test Yourself

Do you have a heart of stone, walls or inner vows? Check for signs and symptoms with this POLL.

A Heart of Stone

I defend my heart with a wall (that keeps out good and bad)

I have a sinful response to hurts or neglect

I tend to shut down my mental capabilities and objectivity

Fear prevents me from opening myself to be vulnerable if it might hurts

Mistrust was formed in my childhood

I isolate from others and push people away

Un-forgiveness prevents healing on the inside even after outward relationship is restored

Bitterness and anger lies hidden behind a warm and friendly exterior

Feeling unworthy and hopeless keeps me from relationships

I have resistance to change for fear of increasing vulnerability

I refuses counsel and ministry because "I believe it will not help"

Triggers habitual resistant behaviors or ways of the flesh

I vowed to "never be like" the one(s) who hurt me

I vowed I will "never act like that"

I vowed to never forgive or let someone off the hook for what happen to me

I avoid feeling real emotions by focusing on compulsive behaviors

I stubbornly resist obvious steps to intimacy in relationships

I vow "I'll never share my true self with anyone again"

I would rather "get even" that reconcile with the perpetrator

I made inner vows not to let the force shield down
I interpret transparency as a potential setup for hurts
I unintentionally block out the healing power of God

_____

_____

_____

_____

_____

_____

_____

_____

_____

_____

_____

_____

Objective: To learn the Importance of Rituals and Their Purpose

LESSON TOPIC 6.2
Walk out Freedom

Ritual are scared. Rituals can help to restore a balance to life. There are numerous ways to create ceremonies to rituals for one occasion or another. Few understand why rituals help in adjusting to change. Even fewer understand the power of ritual to strengthen the bonds that connect us together. The grieving process through rituals can bring great healing to one's soul, mind and body and create an avenue for restoration and wholeness to those who are willing to go through the process.

Rituals can empower people emotionally, mentally, and spiritually. Rituals can be created to heal the mind, heart, and a way of releasing pass hurts, anger, bitterness, build and shame.

LESSON
Do you know where you are in your journey?

Coming to
Yourself

Conception
X

Manhood

The Real You

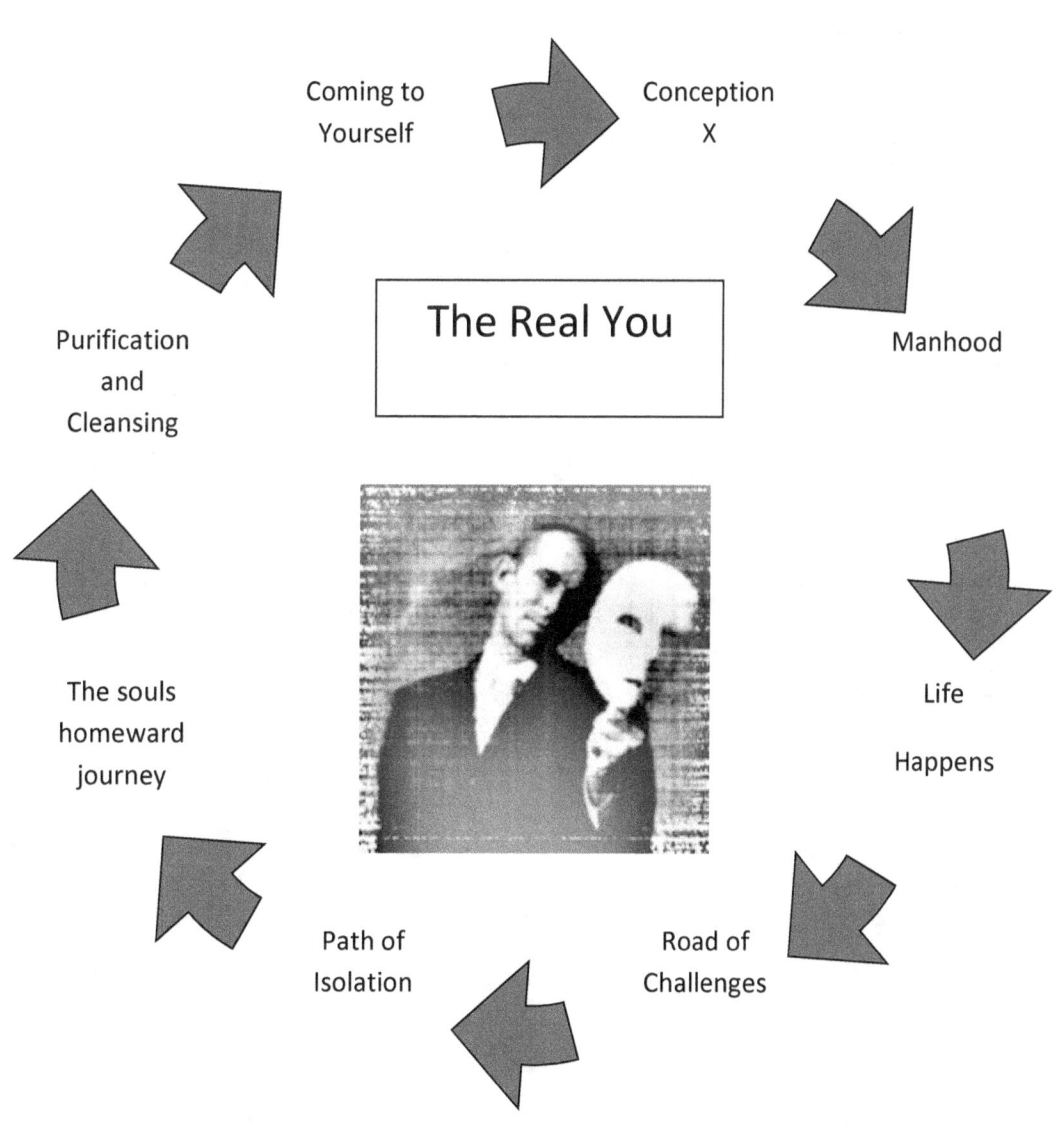

Purification
and
Cleansing

Life

Happens

The souls
homeward
journey

Path of
Isolation

Road of
Challenges

NOTES

REFERENCES

Prayer courtesy by Elijah House, Inc. www.elijahhouse.org

Lesson Topic Definition – Lesson 1.1 - Moral Injury - www.ptsd.va.gov

CONTACT US

You may reach Cynthia Haynes for speaking engagements, events, and/or counseling at:

Rhaynes40@verizon.net

Or

941-704-0988 to set appointment

www.ingramcontent.com/pod-product-compliance
Lightning Source LLC
Chambersburg PA
CBHW081537280526
45788CB00010B/3270